A Companion Anthology to *Literature for Teaching*

Solo Vocal Repertoire for Singers and Teachers of Singers

Mezzo Soprano Edition

by
Christopher Arneson and Lauren Athey-Janka

Inside View Press

Solo Vocal Repertoire for Singers and Teachers of Singers
Mezzo Soprano Edition

by

Christopher Arneson
&
Lauren Athey-Janka

ISBN: 978-0-9910876-4-8

Printed in the United States of America

Inside View Press
Gahanna, Ohio
www.VoxPed.com

Introduction

The intent of this book is to provide tools that will help students and teachers achieve their pedagogic goals. The repertoire we have chosen, along with the technical instructions provided in this book, will guide the teaching of breathing and breath support, phonation, registration, resonance, and articulation. Translations and phonetic transcriptions are provided for each selection to help students explore musical and emotional expression.

For a better understanding of the technical concepts employed in the selection and preparation of the repertoire that is included in this volume, please refer to:

Literature for Teaching: A Guide for Teaching Solo Vocal Repertoire from a Developmental Perspective
by Christopher Arneson with Lauren Athey-Janka, Inside View Press, 2014

Acknowledgements

The authors extend their sincerest thanks to the following people:

Nicolette Biddle
Josh Bodanza
Alexander Brousseau
Andrew Gavin
Lauren Gilmore
Vicky Nooe
Mike Parisi
Kathryn Pepe
Elisabeth Pirolli
Robert Sickles
Dan Sullivan

Solo Vocal Repertoire for Singers and Teachers of Singers
Mezzo Soprano Edition

Table of Contents

I.P.A. GUIDE: VOWELS

Forward vowels:	[i]	cheese	***Back vowels:***	[u]	rude
	[I]	hip		[ʊ]	hook
	[e]	hey		[o]	rope
	[ɛ]	wed		[ɔ]	raw
	[æ]	bad		[ɑ]	father
	[a]	mama			
Central vowels:	[ʌ]	up	***Diphthongs:***	[eɪ]	wait
	[ə]	about		[oʊ]	vote
	[ɝ]	heard, American r		[aɪ]	wine
	[ɒ]	dare, British vocalic r		[aʊ]	couch
	[ɚ]	never, American r		[ɔɪ]	joy
				[ju]	huge

Mixed vowels:	[y]	German: *für*	French: lune
	[Y]	German: *Glück*	
	[ø]	German: *schön*	French: deux
	[œ]	German: *könnte*	French: coeur
French Nasals:	[ɛ̃]	[ɛ] plus nasality	French: *bien* [bjɛ̃] English: fount**ain**
	[ɑ̃]	[ɑ] plus nasality	French: *dans* [dɑ̃] English: h**on**k
	[õ]	[o] plus nasality	French: *bon* [bõ] English: **on**ly
	[œ̃]	[œ] plus nasality	French: *humble* [œ̃blə] English: **un**cle
German Diphthongs:	[aɪ]	German: *meine*	English: mine
	[ao]	German: *Augen*	English: couch
	[ɔø]	German: *Freude*	English: joy
Glottal Stop:	[ʔ]	closure of glottis, as in the expression "uh-oh"	

I.P.A. GUIDE: CONSONANTS

Stop plosives:	[p]	pal	***Nasals:***	[m]	mind
	[b]	back		[n]	narrow
	[t]	teach		[ŋ]	sing
	[d]	down			
	[k]	kangaroo			
	[g]	get			
Fricatives:	[f]	finger	***Lateral:***	[l]	laugh
	[v]	victory			
	[θ]	thin			
	[ð]	that			
	[s]	self			
	[z]	zebra			
	[ʃ]	ship			
	[ʒ]	azure			
	[h]	him			
Glides:	[r]	rose (American English)	***Combined:***	[tʃ]	chip
	[j]	yellow		[dʒ]	jump
	[ʍ]	what, unvoiced			
	[w]	way, voiced			
Trill, Tap, or flip:	[ɾ]	Italian: *moro* (single flip R)			
	[r]	Italian: *ride* (trilled R)			
	[r. r]	Italian: *terra* (prolonged trilled R)			

Enya: [ɲ]	English: onion	Italian: *regno* [reɲɔ]	French: *vignes* [viɲə]
Elya: [ʎ]	English: million	Italian: *figlio* [fiʎɔ]	
French Glide: [ɥ]	French: lui [lɥi] (pronounce [y] then quickly move to [i])		
German ichlaut: [ç]	English: hue	German: *dich* [diç]	
German achlaut: [χ]	German: *nacht* [naχt]		

A Basic Guide to Vocal Exercises for Beginning Singing Teachers

The questions we are asked most frequently concern the use and function of vocal exercises, or *vocalises*. These inquiries often come from young, aspiring voice teachers and singers, so it seems appropriate to discuss their application.

One of the main reasons for using vocal exercises is to establish good singing technique. But while singing teachers likely agree that voice training must address issues of posture and alignment, respiration, phonation, registration, resonation, and articulation, there is little consensus about the specific types of exercises that should be used. Vocal exercises themselves have no intrinsic value; their effectiveness is measured by how they are applied and under what conditions they are used. Vocal exercises can be designed to help singers achieve optimal onset (initiation of the tone), placement, resonance, breath support, phrasing, legato, staccato, agility, range, vowel clarity, consonants, intonation, and coordination of registers (consecutive pitches with similar timbre that are produced with the same vocal mechanism).

Pre-phonatory exercises involving relaxation, posture, and alignment are essential. Working with students to free specific areas of tension, including muscles of the jaw, tongue, and neck, and helping them to understand the importance of a well-aligned body is the first order of business (e.g. spine elongated, neck back, sternum out, pelvis tucked under, knees unlocked).

The goal of a balanced **ONSET**, or the easy, clean initiation of tone, is usually achieved with simple exercises that feature repeated notes with a breath in between each repetition. Voiced consonants facilitate resonance, tonal efficiency, and clean, clear onsets. An audible, aspirate [h] often is used in staccato or panting exercise, quickly moving on to an inaudible, or imaginary [h].

PLACEMENT refers to the physical sensations experienced while singing. Exercises involving nasal consonants, the vowels [e] and [i], and staccato exercises using voiced consonants, often are used to increase the awareness of resonance sensations in the mask (the general area of the cheekbones).

Maximizing **RESONANCE** is one of the chief goals of classical singing; humming often is used as exercise for this purpose. The colloquial, affirmative "mm-hmm" and the nasal consonant [ng], often also are used to increase sensations of resonance, along with the sibilants [s] and [z] followed by vowels.

The coordination of expiration and phonation, called **BREATH SUPPORT** (breath management), can be developed through the use of pulsation exercises on repeated notes (e.g. [a, a, a, a]), staccato, and the *messa di voce* (crescendo-decrescendo). Lip trills also help to develop breath management skills, as do voiced sibilant and fricative consonants [z] and [v].

LEGATO is consistent phonation, uninterrupted by changing pitches or words, and is one of the most desirable aspects of beautiful singing. Glissandos (slides) can be helpful in introducing the idea of legato, followed by intervallic skip, slurring between each skip. Changing vowels on a slow scale or repeated tones with a single vowel also are useful exercises.

STACCATO is produced much in the same way as legato but without sustaining the sound between each note. Simple scales and repeated notes with a vowel preceded by [h] or [b] and simple arpeggiated chords using "hip" and "yuh" teach staccato effectively. Staccato exercises also help to develop onset and breath coordination.

PHRASING is the grouping of notes into specific units for an artistic or technical purposes. Exercises that develop legato and breath management can help to teach phrasing. Sustained scales, arpeggios and exercises with strategically placed breaths also develop the breath control skills necessary for long phrases.

AGILITY, the execution of fast moving passages with clear articulation, accuracy, and freedom, promotes flexibility and coordination and is of primary importance in good singing. Fast arpeggios and ascending/descending scales using the vowels [u] and [a] (or alternating vowels) help to develop agility.

RANGE extension is accomplished by singing ascending and descending scales and arpeggios, using five, eight, nine, eleven, and sixteen tones. A variety of vowels can be used alone and in combination.

VOWEL clarity, unification, equalization, differentiation, and evenness also must be taught. The production of a free, consistent scale throughout the vocal range with distinct, clear vowels on every pitch is paramount to good singing (voice acoustics makes this nearly impossible for women singing their highest pitches). A neutral tongue position from which all other vowels can be produced will help to develop vowel clarity. Simple arpeggios that alternate front and back vowels such as [a-o-i-o], also are useful.

CONSONANTS, especially voiced consonants, frequently are used in vocal exercises to develop coordinated onset and resonance. Scale patterns, repeated notes, arpeggios, and thirds are useful, with consonants articulated on every note. Initial, medial, and final consonants should be included, and paired unvoiced and voiced consonants are beneficial. Exercises using consonants help to create freedom and flexibility in the articulators (jaw, tongue, and lips).

Exercises for the **COORDINATION of REGISTERS** to promote a seamless, consistent vocal scale usually begin in the area just above or below the register break or *passaggio*. A vocalise consisting of two pitches moving slowly from one to the next and modulating up and down through the *passaggio* is helpful. A variety of vowels may be used on short scales, followed by short arpeggios and interval skips. Closed vowels often are used for men in the upper *passaggio* (above Middle-C, also known as C^4) and for women in the lower *passaggio* (also above Middle-C). Alternating between the vowels [u] and [a] can help singers coordinate the registers. Descending arpeggios from the head voice in women and falsetto in men, and the use of sirens (vocal slides) also are beneficial.

Ingo Titze, one of our foremost voice scientists, lists "The Five Best Vocal Warmup Exercises" in Volume 57, No.3, 2001 of the *Journal of Singing*:

- Lip trill and tongue trill
- Two octave pitch glides
- Forward tongue roll and extension
- *Messa di voce* (crescendo-decrescendo)
- Staccato on arpeggios

By taking into account the criteria we use to judge whether a tone is functional and/or beautiful—easy onset, legato, clear diction, bright/dark tone quality, excellent breath management skills—we can make decisions as to which exercises might help students best achieve these goals. Keeping a record of what we see and hear in our initial consultation with a singer can serve as a basis for the vocalises that subsequently are developed and utilized.

Students must understand that a secure singing technique can be achieved through regular use of vocal exercises, which should be described in a simple and objective manner. All exercises should be tailored to serve the needs of individual students; few really are needed, provided every aspect of technique is addressed. Many teachers believe that it is essential to assign a specific sequence of vocal exercises, which often follow the major areas of vocal technique, including posture, respiration, phonation, resonance, support, registration, articulation. While this strategy might prove helpful, it is not required.

There are numerous books of vocalises still in print by the 19th century singing masters, including Sieber, Vaccai, Concone and Marchesi. All were well-known teachers and their exercises, along with those of contemporary authors such as William Vennard, Richard Miller, Oren Brown and James McKinney, can help young teachers get started.

A Vocal Exercise Bibliography

Brown, Oren L. (1996). *Discover Your Voice*. San Diego, CA: Singular Publishing Group, Inc.

Coffin, B. (1980). *Overtones of Bel Canto*. Metuchen, NJ: The Scarecrow Press, Inc.

Concone, J. (1898). *Thirty Daily Exercises for the Voice*. New York: G. Schirmer, Inc.

Garcia, M., II. (1975) *A Complete Treatise on the Art of Singing: Part Two* (D. V. Paschke, Ed. and Trans.). New York: Da Capo Press.

Lamperti, G. B. (1905). *The Techniques of Bel Canto* (M. Heidrich. Ed., T. Baker, Trans.). New York: G. Schirmer.

Marchesi, S. (1970) *Bel Canto: A Theoretical and Practical Vocal Method*. London: Enoch and Sons, Ltd., n.d.; reprint, New York: Dover Publications.

McKinney, J. C. (1982) *The Diagnosis and Correction of Vocal Faults*. Nashville, TN: Broadman Press.

Miller, R. (1986). *The Structure of Singing*. New York: Schirmer Books.

Reid, C. L. (1965). *The Free voice: A Guide to Natural Singing*. New York: Coleman-Ross Company, Inc.

Sieber, Ferdinand (1899). *Thirty-Six Eight-Measure Vocalises for Soprano*: op. 92: Volume 111 of Schirmer's library of music classics.

Sieber, Ferdinand (1899). *Thirty-Six Eight-Measure Vocalises for Mezzo-Soprano*: op. 93: Volume 112 of Schirmer's library of music classics.

Sieber, Ferdinand (1899). *Thirty-Six Eight-Measure Vocalises for Alto*: op. 94: Volume 113 of Schirmer's library of music classics.

Sieber, Ferdinand (1899). *Thirty-Six Eight-Measure Vocalises for Tenor*: op. 95: Volume 114 of Schirmer's library of music classics.

Sieber, Ferdinand (1899). *Thirty-Six Eight-Measure Vocalises for Baritone*: op. 96: Volume 115 of Schirmer's library of music classics.

Sieber, Ferdinand (1899). *Thirty-Six Eight-Measure Vocalises for Bass*: op. 97: Volume 116 of Schirmer's library of music classics.

Vennard, W. (1967). *Singing: The Mechanism and the Technic* (rev. ed.). Boston: Carl Fischer, Inc.

Resta in pace, idolo mio

Italian
Domenico Cimarosa

Respiration and Support

The tempo for this song is indicated as larghetto. To develop the ability to deal with longer phrases, it may be necessary to mark in extra breaths, which can be removed later, after breathing and support skills have been developed.

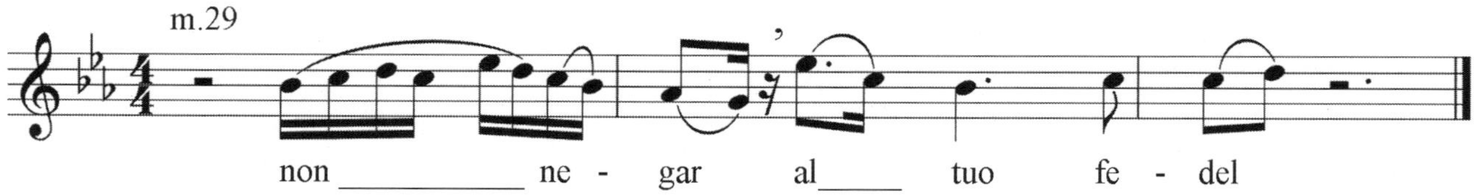

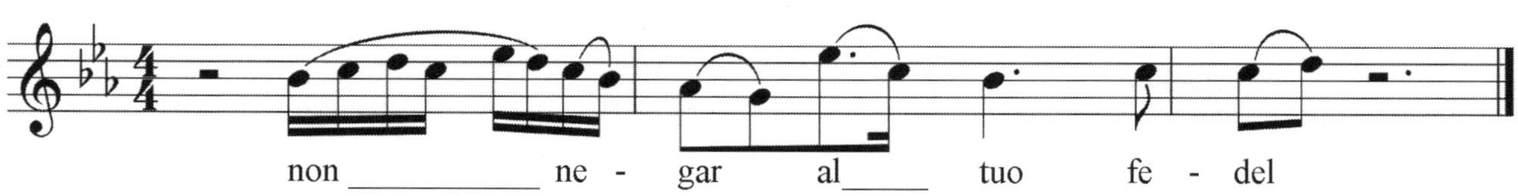

Resonance

Sing the text on E-flat[5], giving special attention to the pharyngeal space needed, to the vowel quality, and to the sensations of resonance.

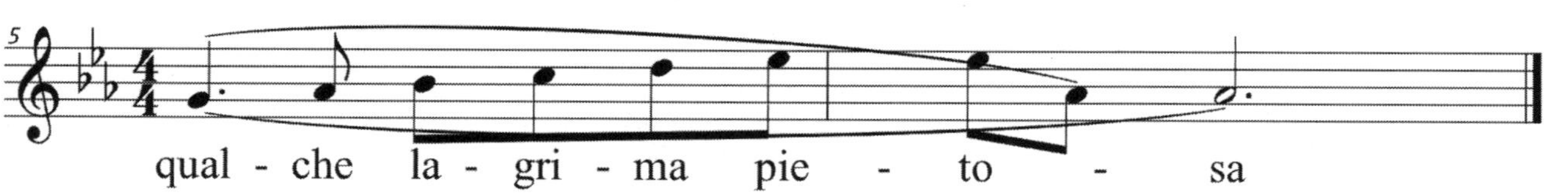

Phonation

Create vocalises that mimic the melismatic passages of this song to teach flexibility, using various vowels. We have created two examples of melismatic vocalises for this purpose.

Below are sample vocalises that mimic the melismatic passages of this song.

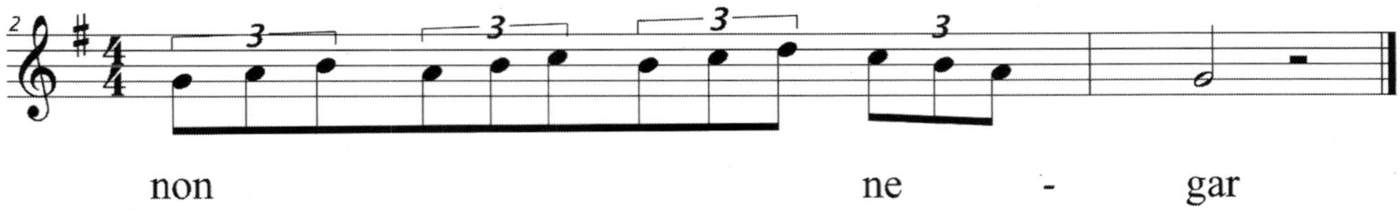

Registration

Create scales from the melody to negotiate B-flat^4 to F^5. Once these scales have been developed, the student can then transition to arpeggios that mimic the melody.

Use ascending scales from the melody, continuing to the scale of F.

Diction and Articulation

Use the exercises below to address the re-articulation of vowels in melismatic passages, which can be applied throughout the song in any difficult passage.

Use the following sequence to address the re-articulation of vowels.

1. Using the rhythm above, pulse on staccati [s] without pitch.

2. Using the rhythm above, pulse on staccati [a] without pitch.

3. Using the rhythm above, sing this melody on the vowel [a] on one pitch.

4. Sing the melody on vowel-to-vowel from "non negare."

5. Now, sing the melody as written.

Phonetic Transcription and Translation of the Text

Resta in pace, idolo mio,
[ˈrɛ.sta in ˈpaː.tʃe ˈiː.do.lo miːo]
Be at peace, my beloved,

Non scordar a chi sei sposa:
[non skɔr.ˈdaːr a ki sɛːi ˈspɔː.za]
do not forget whose bride you are:

Qualche lagrima pietosa
[ˈkwal.ke ˈla.gri.ma pje.ˈtoː.za]
Some tears of pity

Non negare al tuo fedel.
[non ne.ˈgaː.ɾe al tuːo fe.ˈdeːl]
do not deny your faithful one.

Resta in pace, idolo mio

from *Gli Orazi e i Curiazi*

Antonio Simeone Sografi

Domenico Cimarosa
(1749-1801)

ben cantando e molto legato
Curiazio
mp
Re-sta in pa - ce i - do-lo mi - o non scor -
p
dar a chi sei spo - sa
qual - che la-gri-ma pie - to - sa non ne - gar al tu - o fe -
del qual- che la - gri - ma pie - to - sa non ne -

22
23
24
ga - re al tuo fe - del qual-che la - gri-ma pie -
25
26
27
-to-sa qual - che la - gri- ma pie - to-sa non ne-
28
29
30
gar al tu - o fe - del non ne - gar al tuo fe-
31
32
33
mf
poco rit.
del, non ne - gar al tu - o al tuo fe -
poco rit.

p a tempo
del re-sta in pa - ce i - do-lo mi - o non scor-
dar a chi sei spo - sa
p assai
qual - che la-gri-ma pie - to - sa non ne - gar al tu - o fe-
del, non ne - gar al tuo fe - del.
rit.
rit.

Se delitto e l'adorarti

Italian
Alessandro Scarlatti

Respiration and Support
Both rolled and flipped [r] appear frequently in the text of this piece. A rolled [r] is useful for moving air and regulating and managing breath. Sing the melody on a tongue trill. Next, sing melodic passages vowel-to-vowel, inserting rolled [r] before each vowel.

Resonance
This text features double [t:t], double [r:r], [ɲ:ɲ] and ieri [jɛ::ɾi], all of which strengthen the coordination of the raised soft palate. Take an exhilarated breath to lift the soft palate, and then speak slowly through these sounds while maintaining awareness of the vault-like shape of the soft palate.

[ɲ:ɲo - ɲ:ɲo - ɲ:ɲo - ɲ:ɲo]

[it:to - it:to - it:to - it:to]

[jɛ::ɾi - jɛ::ɾi - jɛ::ɾi - jɛ::ɾi]

Phonation
Consonants have a tendency to influence the shape of the vowel that follows. Sing the melody on the vowels found in the text, and then add the consonants while retaining the distinct quality of each vowel.

Sing measures 10-12, eliminating all consonants and only singing the vowels

Next, add the text with the idea of singing consonants as late as possible.

Registration
The vowel sequences found in the text are ideal, and the melody itself is an exercise in registration, because it descends and ascends from the middle voice. Use the examples below to work through both *passaggi*.

The vowels for this five-note descending exercise are taken from measure 4

The vowels for this exercise are taken from measures 7-8

Diction and Articulation
This piece includes some difficult phonemes (distinct sounds in a language), which must be practiced in speech to achieve fluid transition from sound-to-sound.

Practice the double consonants [t:t] and consonant cluster [r:t].

Delitto è l'adorarti
[de:ˈlit:to ɛ la:do:ˈɾa:r:ti]

Practice the consonant cluster [gr] and double consonants [r:r].

Grande error
[gran:de ɛr:‘ro:r]

Two consecutive dental consonants may be difficult for a beginner student. Inserting a shadow vowel between [n] and [r] will ease articulation. Eventually the two dental consonants will be created in the vowel space taught by the shadow vowel.

son rea
[so:n (ə) ˈrɛ::a]

Phonetic Transcription and Translation of the Text

Se delitto è l’adorarti,
[se de.ˈlit.to ɛ la.do.ˈɾaːr.ti]
If it is a crime to love you,

io son rea d’un grande error,
[iːo soːn ˈrɛː.a dun ˈgran.de ɛr.ˈroːr]
then I am guilty of a great error,

tu signor de miei voleri
[tu siɲːˈɲoːr de ˈmjɛːi vo.ˈleː.ɾi]
you are the master of my desires

e tiranno di pensieri;
[e ti.ˈɾan.no di pɛn.ˈsjɛː.ɾi]
and tyrant of my thoughts;

altra colpa che l’amarti
[ˈal.tra ˈkol.pa ke la.ˈmaːr.ti]
no fault other than loving you

non ritrovo nel mio cor.
[non ɾiːˈtrɔː.vo nel miːo kɔːr]
do I find in my heart.

Page intentionally left blank to facilitate page turns

Se delitto è l'adorarti

Alessandro Scarlatti
(1660-1725)

7
8
rar - ti, io son re - a son rea d'un grande er - ror, io son
p
9
10
re - a, son rea d'un grande er —ror tu si - gnor de' miei vo -
11
12
le - ri e ti - ran - no di pen - sie - ri al - tra col - pa che l'a -

13
cresc.
14
mar - ti al - tra col - pa che_ l'a - mar - ti non ri - tro - vo non ri -
cresc.
15
16
tro - vo nel mio cor non ri - tro - vo nel mio cor
17
18

19
20
Se de - lit - to è l'a - do - rar - ti
21
22
Se de - lit - to è l'a - do - rar - ti io son re - a, son
23
24
ten.
25
rea d'un grand' er - ror io son re - a son rea d'un grand' er - ror.
f

Und kommt er nicht mehr zurück?

German
Johannes Brahms

Respiration and Support
Brahms' handling of rhythm often is complex, creating an unpredictable pattern and rhythm for breathing. The breath can easily lock in this situation. Notice the difference in the first seven measures of this song. The first breaths are in a predictable pattern; the following two breaths are more unexpected.

Using a colored pencil, create a visual road map for breathing by marking all breaths in your own score.

Resonance
Mixed vowels will encourage consistent resonance because a balance between the position of the tongue, larynx and lips, which leads to a naturally resonant tone, is inherent within the vowel. This can be taught through the following steps:

1. a position of [i] with the tongue
2. a position of [u] with the lips
3. a feeling of [o] in the throat

For example, the word *zurück* requires this type of positioning.

Phonation
Teaching the uvular [r] as a vowel can be an effective tool for maintaining legato. The uvular [r] can be taught through the use of the British (ɒ) as in *dare, where, nor, etc*. Practice these words with a British accent, then transition to German words found in the song:

mehr- meːɒ
er- ʔeːɒ
nimmer- nɪːmɒ

Registration
It is essential to develop the lower *passaggio* in the mezzo soprano voice. This piece includes descending phrases with the pitch D^4 appearing frequently. In this pitch area, the mouth should not be wide open. The closed vowels in the first verse, which encourage balance, should influence the vowels in the second verse.

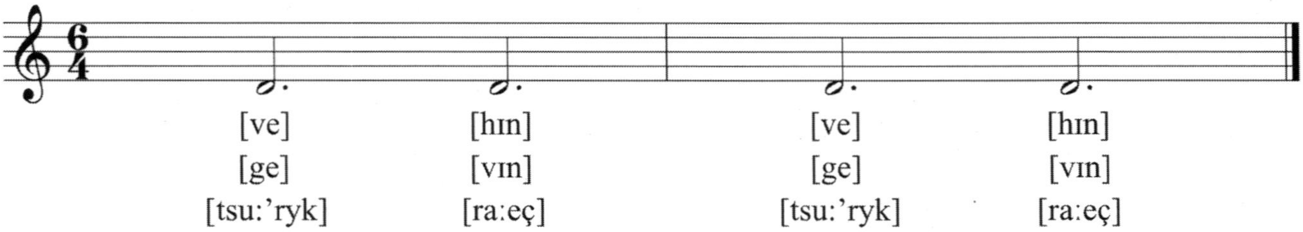

Diction and Articulation

The closed [o] in German is difficult for most American speakers because there is no diphthong. The lips are rounded and the cheeks are indented. Examples are found in the text:

kommt [kɔmt]   *tot* [tot]

Practice alternating the open and the closed o.

[ɔ] to [o] to [ɔ] to [o]

Notice that many German words end with a *schwa* sound: [ə]. This is a unique speech sound in German that requires practice. Many American singers incorrectly use the wrong sounds. This was Lindsey Christiansen's[1] explanation of *Schwa*:

After bright vowels, shaded toward [ɛ]: liebe, schwebe
After rounded vowels, shaded toward rounded [ə]: möchte, rufe
When these sounds appear at the end of a word: en, el, es, et, er, shaded toward darker [ə]: Himmel, Mutter

Phonetic Transcription and Translation of the Text

Und kommt er nicht mehr zurück?
[ʔʊnt kɔmt ʔeːɐ̯ nɪçt meːɐ̯ tsu.ˈrʏk]
And will he not come back?

Er ist Tot, o weh!
[ʔeːɐ̯ ʔɪst toːt ʔoː veː]
He is dead, oh woe!

In dein Todesbett geh'
[ʔɪn daːen ˈ dəs.ˌbɛt geː]
Go to your death-bed,

Er kommt ja nimmer zurück.
[ʔeːɐ̯ kɔmt jaː nɪ.mɐ tsu.ˈrʏk]
he will never come back.

Sein Bart war so weiß wie Schnee,
[zaːen bart vaːɐ̯ zoː vaːes viː ʃneː]
His beard was white as snow,

Sein Haupt dem Flachse gleich:
[zaːen haːupt deːm ˈfla.ʃsə glaːeç]
his hair as fair as flax:

Er ist hin, er ist hin,
[ʔeːɐ̯ ʔɪst hɪn ʔeːɐ̯ ʔɪst hɪn]
he is gone, he is gone,

Und kein Leid bringt Gewinn:
[ʔʊnt kaːen laːet brɪŋkt gə.ˈvɪn]
and our sorrow is futile:

Gott helf' ihm ins Himmelreich!
[gɔt hɛlf ʔiːm ʔɪns ˈhɪ.məl.ˌraːeç]
God have mercy on his soul!

[1] Professor Christiansen was a prominent singing teacher who spent most of her career teaching at Westminster Choir College

Und kommt er nicht mehr zurück?

V. from *Ophelia-Lieder*

William Shakespeare
Translated by
August Wilhelm von Schlegel

Johannes Brahms
(1833-1897)

* introduction added to aid young singers

13 14 15 16
Bart war so weiß wie Schnee, sein Haupt dem Flach - se gleich:

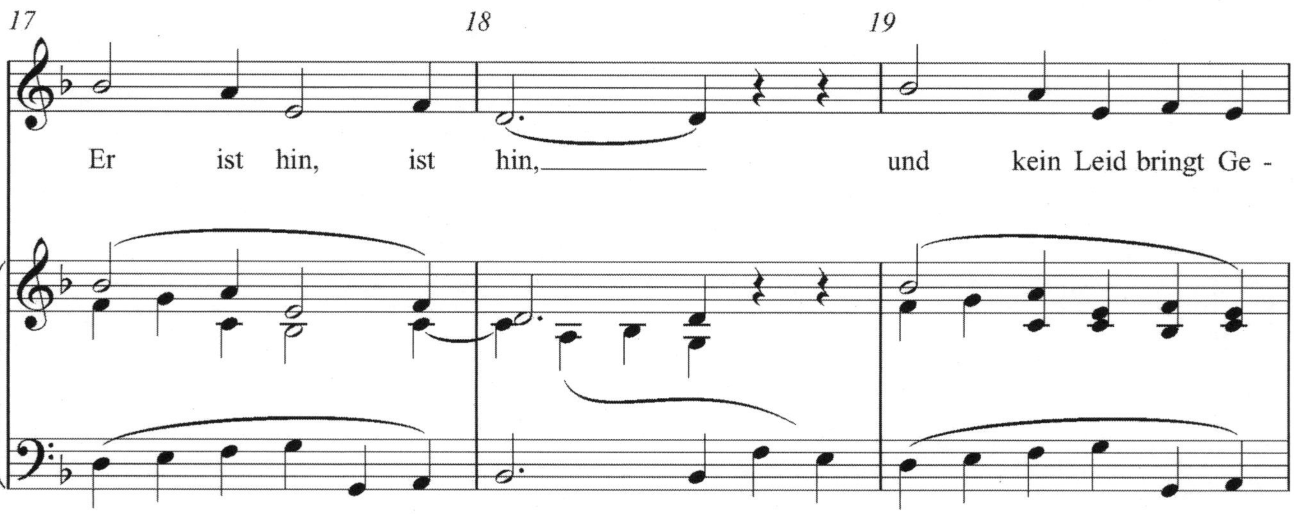
17 18 19
Er ist hin, ist hin, und kein Leid bringt Ge -

20 21 22
winn; Gott helf' ihm ins Him - mel-reich, ins Him - mel-reich!

Hans und Grete

German
Gustav Mahler

Respiration and Support
Practice an inhalation with a long sniff to prepare the larynx and the soft palate for the vertical space required. Imagine a sensation of cool air behind the eyes to increase awareness of the soft palate.

Resonance
Sing the melody on [ja-ua]. [J] is a tongue glide, and [u] is a lip glide. Both can help to balance resonance.

Phonation
The vowels [ʊ] and [e] have very different colors and must be distinct. Vowels easily can be influenced by the consonants that precede or follow them. Practice the distinction between these two German vowels within the word "*Jucche*!" [jʊχ.ˈhe]

[ʊ]: the lips are round and protruded and there is a great amount of vertical space in the mouth

[e]: the position of the tongue is forward and arched high, similar to the position of the tongue in [i] in English

Registration
Practice the intervals at the opening of the piece, using [ng], to stabilize to the position of the larynx and to assist in creating consistent registration and resonance.

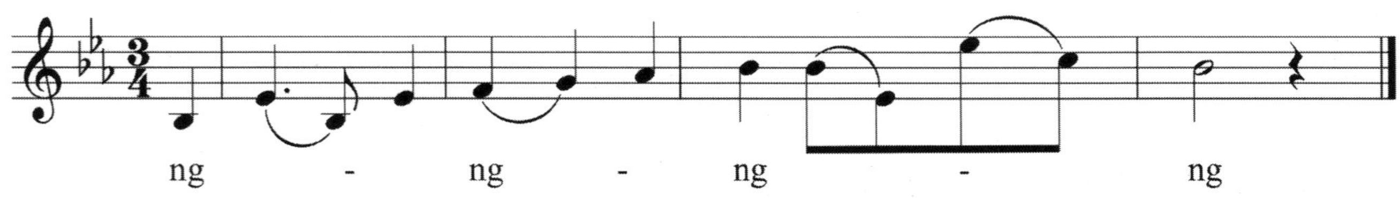

The two versions of this exercise will release the tongue for the lower *passaggio*. Repeat this pattern descending by half steps.

1. Tongue between lips (raspberry trill)
2. [ða - ðe - ði - ðo - ðu]

Diction and Articulation
This song contains word pronunciations that are challenging. Practice the following words, paying special attention to the *ich-laut* and the *ach-laut*:

Liepchen - [ʻliːp.çən]
Glücklich – [ˈglʏk.lɪç]
Jucche- [jʊχ.ˈhe]
Suchte- [ˈzʊχ.tə]

Phonetic Transcription and Translation of the Text

Ringel, ringel Reih'n!
[ˈrɪːŋəl ˈrɪːŋəl raːen]
Ring-around-a-rosy!

Wer fröhlich ist, der schlinge sich ein!
[veːɐ̯ ˈfrøː.lɪç ʔɪst deːɐ̯ ˈʃlɪ.ŋə zɪç ʔaːen]
Whoever is joyful may join in our dance!

Wer sorgen hat, der lass' sie daheim!
[veːɐ̯ ˈzɔr.gən hat deːɐ̯ las ziː daːˈhaːem]
Whoever has troubles can leave them at home!

Wer ein liebes Liebchen küßt,
[veːɐ̯ ʔaːen ˈliːbəs ˈliːp.çən kʏst]
Whoever is kissed by their beloved,

Wie glücklich der ist!
[viː ˈglʏk.lɪç deːɐ̯ ʔɪst]
How lucky they are!

Ei, Hänsel, du hast ja kein's!
[ʔaːe ˈhɛn.səl duː hast jaː kaːens]
Hey Hansel, you don't have anyone!

So suche dir ein's!
[zoː ˈzuː.χə diːɐ̯ ʔaːens]
So go seek one out!

Ein schönes Liebchen,
[ʔaːen ˈʃøː.nəs ˈliːp.çən]
A beautiful sweetheart

das ist was Fein's. Juchhe!
[das ʔɪst vas faːens jʊχ.ˈheː]
is something wonderful. Hurray!

Ringel, ringel Reih'n!
[ˈrɪːŋəl ˈrɪːŋəl raːen]
Ring-around-a-rosy!

Ei, Gretel, was stehst denn so allein?
[ʔaːe ˈgreː.təl vas ʃteːst dɛn zoː ʔa.ˈlaːen]
Hey, Gretel, why are you standing all alone?

Guckst doch hinüber zum Hänseleín!?
[gʊkst dɔχ hɪn.ˈyː.bɐ tsum ˈhɛn.sə.laːen]
Look over there at little Hansel!?

Und ist doch der Mai so grün?
[ʔʊnt ʔɪst dɔχ deːɐ̯ maːe zoː gryːn]
And isn't it the May so green?

Und die Lüfte sie zieh'n!
[ʔʊnt diː ˈlʏf.tə ziː tsiːn]
And how the breezes they blow!

Ei, seht doch den dummen Hans!
[ʔaːe zeːt dɔχ deːn ˈdʊ.mən hans]
Hey, look at that dumb Hans!

Wie er rennet zum Tanz!
[viː ʔeːɐ̯ ˈrɛ.nət tsʊm tants]
How he rushes to the dance floor!

Er suchte eine Liebchen Juchhe!
[ʔeːɐ̯ ˈzʊχ.tə ˈʔaːe.nə ˈliːp.çən jʊχ.ˈheː]
He was looking for a sweetheart, hurray!

Er fand's! Juchhe!
[ʔeːɐ̯ fants jʊχ.ˈheː]
He has found one! Hurray!

Ringel, ringel Reih'n!
[ˈrɪːŋəl ˈrɪːŋəl raːen]
Ring-around-a-rosy!

Page intentionally left blank to facilitate page turns

Hans und Grete

Volkslied

Gustav Mahler
(1860-1911)

Im gemächlichen Walzertempo

Etwas zurückhaltend
Wer ein lie - bes Lieb - chen küsst, wie glück - lich der ist!
Ei, Häns - chen, du hast ja kein's!
So su - che dir ein's!
Ein lie - bes
rit.
accel.
p
f
tr

Lieb-chen, das ist was Fein's. Juch - he! Juch - he!
ff
f
mf
mf
p
Rin - gel, rin - gel
p
Etwas langsamer.
Reih'n! Ei, Gret - chen, was stehst denn so al - lein?
pp

a tempo
Guckst doch hin - ü - ber zum Hän - se - lein!?
rit.
rit.
rit.
ff
a tempo
tr
tr
mf

p rit.
accel.
mf
Und ist doch der Mai so grün!? Und die Lüf - te sie
p rit
accel.
mf
zieh'n! Ei, seht doch den dum - men Hans! Wie er ren - net zum
p rit
a tempo
ff
Tanz! Er such - te ein Lieb - chen, Juch - he! Er fand's! Juch -

f
p
75
76
77
78
79
he! Juch - he! Juch - he! Juch - he! Rin - gel,
f
p
p sich verlierend
80
dimin.
81
82
83
84
rin - gel Reih'n! Rin - gel Reih'n! Rin - gel
dimin.
p
85
86
87
88
89
Reih'n! Reih'n!
pp

Fêtes Galantes

French
Reynaldo Hahn

Setting up a method of studying the language separate from the music and rhythm is essential, and the teaching of the I.P.A. from the chart included in this volume is very important. It also can be very helpful for the teacher to record the text for the student (assuming he or she has excellent French diction).

N.B. The marking *"très crâne et avec élégance"* indicates to sing with a great deal of vigor and with elegance.

Respiration and Support
Sing the melody [si], [zi], [sa], and [za], which will prevent the breath from locking

Resonance
Sing [l], with the jaw released and the tip of the tongue touching the alveolar ridge, on the first syllable of each word to keep the back of the tongue released and to avoid creating false resonance. Next, sing the melody remembering the sensations of [l].

Phonation
Practice quick renewal of breaths (catch breaths) between onsets, which teaches the throat to remain open and relaxed, no matter how quick the inhalation must be.

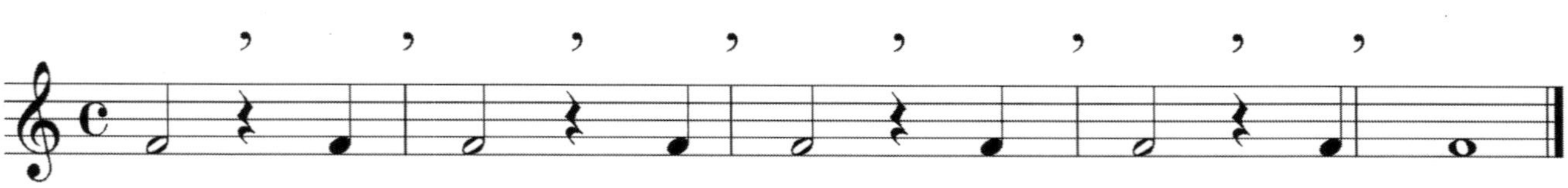

Registration

To practice the octave leaps in measures 29-32, use lips trills then [ga] + [ly] to help coordinate registration. Continue this exercise up to F-sharp ^{5} or G^5, and then descend back down to the original octave.

Diction and Articulation

This song is comprised of three verses, each of which has many words. Follow these steps to learn the text and articulation:

1. The words should be practiced first, out of rhythm, paying attention to the smooth transitions from syllable to syllable. This is achieved by efficiency and fluidity in the muscles of articulation.

2. Use an exaggerated sense of legato at a slow tempo, continuing to practice speaking through the text.

3. Work up to a moderate tempo. Notes and rhythm should be added only after this is achieved.

Phonetic Transcription and Translation of the Text

Les donneurs de sérénades
[lɛ dɔ.nør də se.ɾe.na.də]
The singers of serenades

Et les belles écouteuses
[e lɛ bɛ.lə.‿ ze.ku.tø.zə]
and the lovely listeners

Échangent des propos fades
[e.ʃɑ̃.ʒə dɛ pɾɔ.po fa.də]
exchange sweet nothings

Sous les ramures chanteuses.
[su lɛ ɾa.my.ɾə ʃɑ̃.tø.zə]
beneath singing branches.

C'est Tircis |et c'est Aminte,
[sɛ tiɾ.sis e sɛ.‿ta.mɛ̃.tə]
It's Thyrsis and Amyntas

Et c'est l'éternel Clitandre,
[e sɛ le.tɛɾ.nɛl kli.tɑ̃.dɾə]
and the eternal Clytander,

Et c'est Damis qui pour mainte
[e sɛ da.mis ki puɾ mɛ̃.tə]
and there's Damis who writes, for

Cruelle fait maint vers tendre.
[kry.ɛ.lə fɛ mɛ̃ vɛɾ tɑ̃.dɾə]
cruel women, many tender verses.

Leurs courtes vestes de soie,
[løɾ kuɾ.tə vɛs.tə də swa]
Their short jackets of silk,

Leurs longues robes à queues,
[løɾ lõ.gə ɾɔ.bə.‿za kø]
their long gowns with trains,

Leur élégance, leur joie
[lø.‿ɾe.le.gɑ̃.sə løɾ ʒwa]
their elegance, their joy

Et leurs molles ombres bleues
[e løɾ mɔ.lə.‿zõ.bɾə blø]
and their soft blue shadows

Tourbillonnent dans l'extase
[tuɾ.bi.jɔ.nə dɑ̃ lɛks.ta.zə]
whirl around in the ecstasy

D'une lune rose et grise,
[dy.nə ly.nə ɾo.‿ze gɾi.zə]
of a pink and grey moon,

Et la mandoline jase
[e la mɑ̃.dɔ.li.nə ʒa.zə]
and the mandolin babbles

Parmi les frissons de brise.
[paɾ.mi le fɾi.sõ də bɾi.zə]
amid shivers stirred by the breeze.

Fêtes Galantes

Paul Verlaine

Reynaldo Hahn
(1874-1947)

11
12
13
fa - des Sous les ra - mu - res chan-teu - ses.
8va
p
14
15
16
(8)
17
18
maniéré
19
C'est Tir-cis et c'est A - min - te,
sf
p
dim.
20
21
22
Et c'est l'é - ter-nel Cli - tan - dre, Et c'est Da-mis, qui, pour main - te Cru-

23
24
25
el - le fait maint vers ten - dre...
mf grazioso
26
27
28
finement
Leurs cour-te ves - tes de
pp
29
30
31
soi - e, Leurs lon-gues ro-bes à queu - es, Leur é-lé gan - ce, leur
pp

molto dim.
rall. (senza respiro)
joi - - - e Et leurs mol-les om-bres bleues
rall.
p a tempo
Tour-bil-lon - nent dans l'ex-ta - se d'u-ne lu - ne ro - se et
pp
p
poco ritenuto
gri - - - - - - se.
a tempo mf
Et la man-do-li - ne
pp
a tempo
sf
p

pp (en fausset)
sans ralentir
ja - se Par - mi les fris-sons de bri - - - - - - -
se.
mf
p
8va
(8)
dim.
sf

Ce que je suis sans toi

French
Charles Gounod

Respiration and Support

Nasal vowels can be helpful in balancing registration. For example, they can help avoid an overly dark or back tone in the upper *passaggio*. Practice this exercise through the passaggio up to F^5.

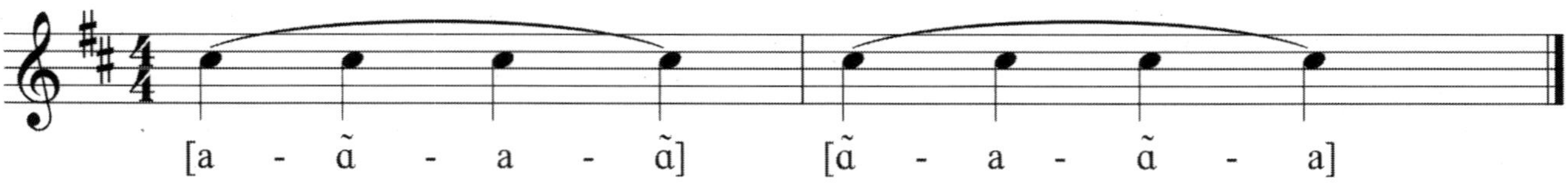

Next, apply this concept to the vocal line.

Resonance

To explore the brighter timbre of the French language, use vocalises that create sensations above the roof of the mouth, high in the skull, and the cheekbones. The quality of [ng] followed by a vowel can result in the correct balance of resonance. In the following exercise, spring the palate up from [ng] into the vowel.

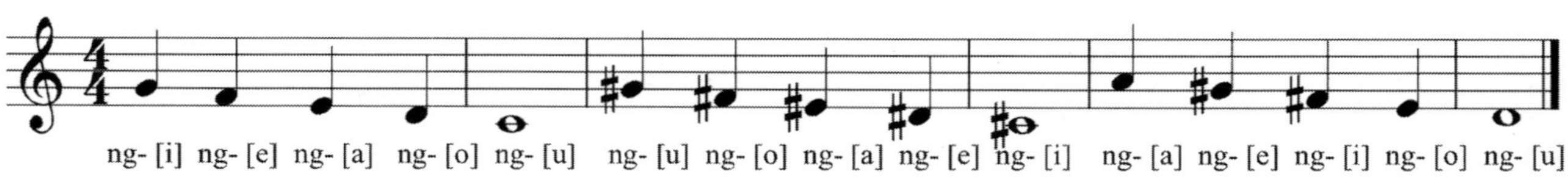

Phonation

The text of this song is full of excellent opportunities to develop good habits of phonation. The recurring dental [l] helps the vocal folds to approximate (closing the glottis) and vibrate. Practice this exercise, and then apply this idea to every [l] in the text.

Sing [l], maintaining consistent legato and vibrancy.

Sing [l] to [a], maintaining fluidity.

Reverse this exercise to sing the vowel first, then [l].

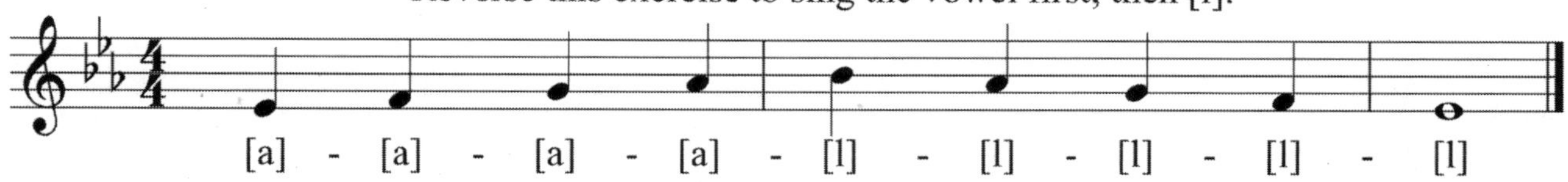

Registration

Because the places to breathe in this song are unpredictable, practice without words and without pitch, taking the breaths on the correct beats. The breathing has to be rhythmic and of excellent quality. Treat this as a study of breath as it relates to rhythm.

Diction and Articulation

Teaching pronunciation of unfamiliar French nasal vowels through the use of American words can be very helpful.

[ɛ̃] fount***ain***
[œ̃] ***un***cle
[ɑ̃] h***on***k
[õ] ***on***ly

Phonetic Transcription and Translation of the Text

Ce qu'est le lierre sans l'ormeau
[sə kɛ lə ljɛ.ɾə sɑ̃ ll l'orm*Just as*
ivy without the elm

Qui fut l'appui de son enfance,
[ki fy la.pɥi də sõ.‿nɑ̃.fɑ̃.sə]
that was its support of its infancy,

Lui donnant dans chaque rameau
[lɥi dɔ.nɑ̃ dɑ̃ ʃa.kə ɾa.mo]
giving it, with each branch

Un échelon pour sa croissance;
[œ̃.‿ne.ʃɔ.lõ puɾ sa kɾwa.sɑ̃.sə]
a step for its growth;

Voilà ce que je suis sans toi;
[vwa.la sə kə ʒə sɥi sɑ̃ twa]
that is what I am without you;

Par pitié, garde - moi ta foi!
[paɾ pi.tjɛ gaɾ.də. mwa ta fwa]
for pity's sake, may your faith protect me!

L'oiseau qui vole en gazouillant
[lwa.zo ki vɔ.‿lɑ̃ ga.zu.jɑ̃]
The bird that sings in flight

Vers les demeures éternelles
[vɛɾ lɛ də.mø.ɾə.‿ze.tɛɾ.nɛ.lə]
towards the eternal dwellings

Et dont soudain |un plomb sanglant
[e dõ su.dɛ̃ œ̃ plõ sɑ̃.glɑ̃]
and is suddenly wounded by a shot

Est venu fracasser les ailes,
[ɛ və.ny fɾa.ka.se lɛ.‿zɛ.lə]
shattering its wings,

Voilà ce que je suis sans toi;
[vwa.la sə kə ʒə sɥi sɑ̃ twa]
that is what I am without you;

Par pitié, garde - moi ta foi!
[paɾ pi.tje gaɾ.də. mwa ta fwa]
for pity's sake, may your faith protect me!

Un frêle esquif parmi les flots
[œ̃ fɾɛ.‿lɛs.kif paɾ.mi lɛ flo]
A frail boat among the waves

Pendant une nuit ténébreuse,
[pɑ̃.dɑ̃.‿ty.nə nɥi te.ne.bɾø.zə]
during a dark night,

Sans gouvernail, sans matelots,
[sɑ̃ gu.vɛɾ.naj sɑ̃ ma.tə.lo]
without a rudder, without sailors,

Au sein de la mer orageuse,
[o sɛ̃ də la mɛ.‿ɾɔ.ra.ʒø.zə]
in the folds of the stormy sea;

Voilà ce que je suis sans toi;
[vwa.la sə kə ʒə sɥi sɑ̃ twa]
that is what I am without you;

Par pitié, garde - moi ta foi!
[paɾ pi.tjɛ gaɾ.də. mwa ta fwa]
for pity's sake, may your faith protect me!

Page intentionally left blank to facilitate page turns

Ce que je suis sans toi

Louis de Peyre

Charles Gounod
(1818-1893)

Moderato con moto

13
14
15
ce, Voi - là ce que je suis sans toi,
p cresc.
dim.
p
16
17
18
19
voi - là ce que je suis sans toi. Par pi - tié, gar - de moi ta foi! Par pi -
cresc.
dim.
p
20
21
22
23
tié gar - de moi ta foi!
colla voce
cresc.
Ped.

24
25
26
27
L'oi-seau qui vole en ga-zou-illant Vers les de-
dim.
p
Ped.
28
29
30
meu-res é-ter-nel - les Et dont sou-dain un plomb san-
Ped.
31
32
33
glant Est ve-nu fra-cas-ser les ai - les,
cresc.
dim.
p cresc.
dim.
Ped.

34
35
36
37
Voi-là ce que je suis sans toi,
voi-là ce que je suis sans toi,
Par pi-
p
cresc.
38
39
40
41
tié, gar-de moi ta foi!
Par pi-tié gar-de moi ta foi!
dim.
p
colla voce
a tempo
42
43
44
45
cresc.
dim.
p
Ped.
Ped.

46
47
48
Un frêle es - quif par - mi les flots Pen-dant u - ne nuit té - né breu -
Ped.
49
50
51
-se, Sans gou-ver - nail, Sans ma - te - lots Au sein de
cresc.
52
53
54
la mer o - ra - geu - se, Voi - là ce que je suis sans
dim.
p cresc.
p

toi, voi-là ce que je suis sans toi. Par pi-tié, gar-de moi ta
cresc.
dim.
foi! Par pi-tié, gar-de moi ta
p
pp
colla voce
foi!
cresc.
dim.

I Dreamt that I Dwelt in Marble Halls

English
Michael Balfe

Respiration and Support
Sing the melody through a straw using a small [u]. Next, take the straw out of the mouth but maintain the same position. The lips will buzz, and the support muscles in the lower abdomen should move up and back toward the spine.

Resonance
The sensation inside of the mouth should be one of great space, with a high and wide arch created by a lifted soft palate. This exercise will help to develop the flexible and raised position of the soft palate. On the melody of the song, sing [ki ke ki ka].

Phonation
Practice singing this song on [hʌm-mʌm-ma] to encourage consistent vibrancy in the tone.

Registration
Mimicking an owl, sigh [u] from one octave above the starting pitch.

N.B. [ð] is voiced as in the world *that*, which is found in the text. In the exercise below, slide from [u] into phonemes that follow:

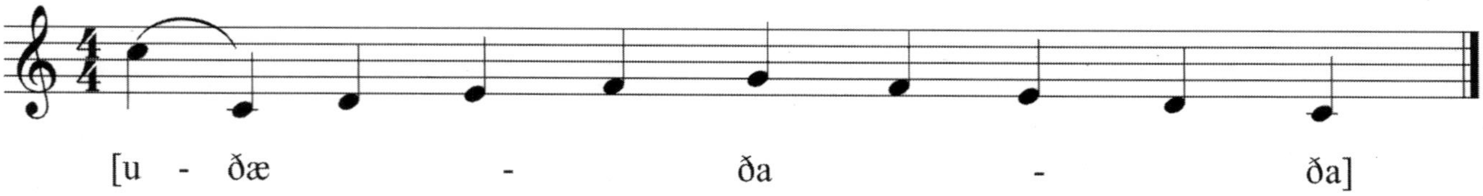

Diction and Articulation

The consonant clusters in this song may present challenges for some students. For example, the words *dreamt* and *pride* include these clusters.

Practice the consonants separately, pointing out the "place" of pronunciation.

For example:

*Dr*eamt
[d]- lingual alveolar- tongue against the teeth
[r]- lingual alveolar- rolled non-fricative [r], blade of tongue against the alveolar ridge
*Pr*ide
[p]- bilabial- top and bottom lips are used
[r]- lingual alveolar- rolled non-fricative [r], blade of tongue against the alveolar ridge

Phonetic Transcription of the Text

I dreamt that I dwelt in marble halls,
[a:ɪ dɹɛm*pt* ðæt a:ɪ dwɛlt ɪn 'mɑɐ̯.bəl hɔlz]

with vassals and serfs at my side,
[wɪð 'væ.səlz ænd sɜfs æt ma:ɪ sa:ɪd]

And of all who assembled within those walls
[ænd ɑv ɔl hu ə.'sɛm.bəld wɪð.'ɪn ðo:ʊz wɔlz]

that I was the hope and the pride.
[ðæt a:ɪ wɑz ðʌ ho:ʊp ænd ðʌ pɹa:ɪd]

I had riches too great to count, could boast
[a:ɪ hæd 'rɪt͡ʃ.ɪz tu gɹe:ɪt tu ka:ʊnt kʊd bo:ʊst]

Of a high ancestral name,
[ɑv ʌ ha:ɪ æn.'sɛs.tɹəl ne:ɪm]

But I also dreamt, which pleased me most
[bʌt a:ɪ 'ɔl.so:ʊ dɹɛm*pt* ʍɪt͡ʃ plizd mi mo:ʊst]

That you loved me still the same.
[ðæt ju lʌvd me stɪl ðʌ se:ɪm]

I dreamt that suitors sought my hand;
[a:ɪ dɹɛm*pt* ðæt 'su.tɐz sɔt ma:ɪ hænd]

that knights, upon bended knee,
[ðæt na:ɪts ə.'pɑn 'bɛnd.əd ni]

And with vows no maiden heart could withstand,
[ænd wɪð va:ʊz no:ʊ 'me:ɪd.ən hɑɐ̯ kʊd wɪð.'stænd]

they pledg'd their faith to me.
[ðeːɪ plɛd͡ʒd ðɛɐ̯ feːɪθ tu mi]

And I dreamt that one of that noble host
[ænd aːɪ dɹɛm*p*t ðæt wʌn ɑv ðæt 'noːʊbəl hoːʊst]

Came forth my hand to claim;
[keːɪm fɔɐ̯θ maːɪ hænd tu kleːɪm]

But I also dreamt, which pleased me most,
[bʌt aːɪ 'ɔl.soːʊ dɹɛm*p*t ʍɪt͡ʃ plizd mi moːʊst]

That you loved me still the same.
[ðæt ju lʌvd mi stɪl ðʌ seːɪm]

Page intentionally left blank to facilitate page turns

I Dreamt That I Dwelt in Marble Halls

from *The Bohemian Girl*

Alfred Bunn

Michael Balfe
(1808-1870)

21 22 23 24 25 26
vas - sals and serfs at my side, And of all who as - sem-bled with-
knights, up - on bend- ed knee, And with vows no mai - den
27 28 29 30 31 32
in those walls that I was the hope and the pride. I had
heart could with- stand, they pled-ged their faith to me. And I
33 34 35 36 37 38
ri - ches too great to count, could boast of a high an - ces - tral
dreamt that one of that no - ble host, Came forth my hand to

name,___ But I al - so dreamt, which pleas'd me most, that you loved me
claim;___ But I al - so dreamt,_ which charm'd me most, that you loved me
pp
still the same, that you loved me, you loved_ me still_ the same, that you loved me, you
still the same, that you loved me, you loved_ me still_ the same, that you loved me, you
1.
loved_ me still_ the same.
loved_ me

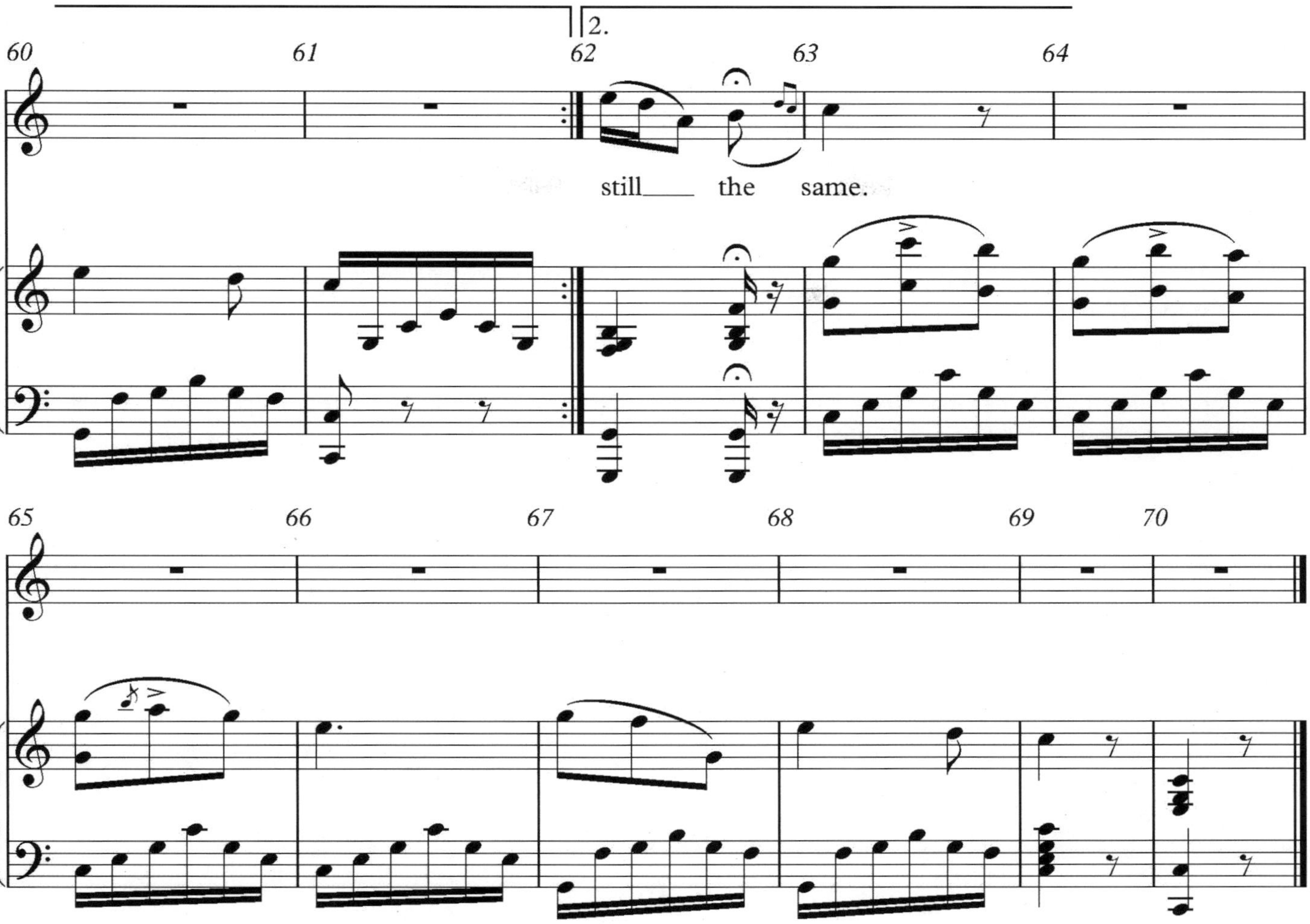
2.
60
61
62
63
64
still___ the same.
65
66
67
68
69
70

Late Summer

English
Peter Warlock

Respiration and Support

This song is full of long phrases that require proper breath support. The first line of the song includes several unvoiced consonants, in which the glottis remains open (*f*ield*s*, *f*ull, *s*ummer, *st*ill). To ensure that the glottis has proper closure after the first phrase of the song, place the palm of the hand in front of the mouth while singing. If a high amount of exhaled breath is felt, try to reduce it by excluding the unvoiced consonants.

Resonance

Use various voiced consonants to balance resonance. These initial consonants will prepare a vowel with balanced *chiaroscuro*.

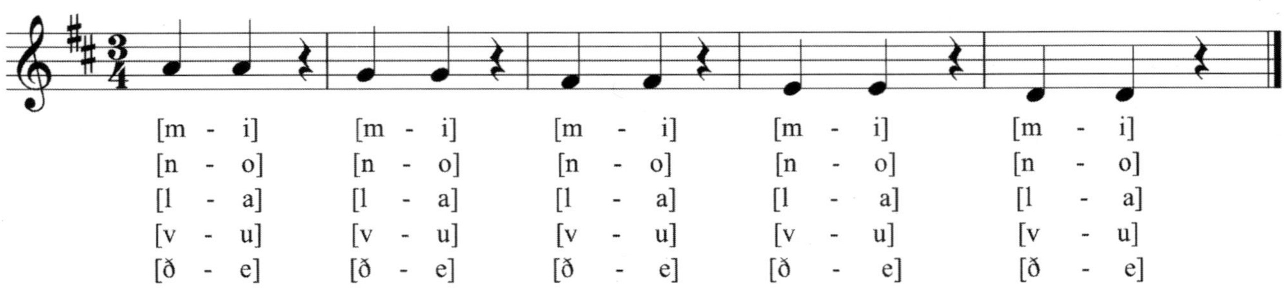

Phonation

The voice is exposed when singing long phrases, so it is particularly important to listen for consistent vibrancy and clear vowels.

This exercise will train the positioning of the vocal tract and vibrancy of the vocal folds:

> First, to encourage the correct position and shape of the vocal folds and vocal tract and to maintain vibrancy, sing the melody through a straw.
>
> Next, use a straw to sing the first note of a phrase, and then remove the straw while continuing to sing with the same basic sound (without a breath between the straw phonation and the first word).

Registration

The range of this piece is about an octave-and-a-half. To coordinate registration, yawn with an open, relaxed throat, from your highest comfortable pitch to your lowest comfortable pitch, using the vowels [a], [e], [i], [o] or [u]. Next, yawn from the lowest comfortable pitch in your range to the highest comfortable pitch, using the same vowels. Finally, extract leaps from the song and practice using the same technique.

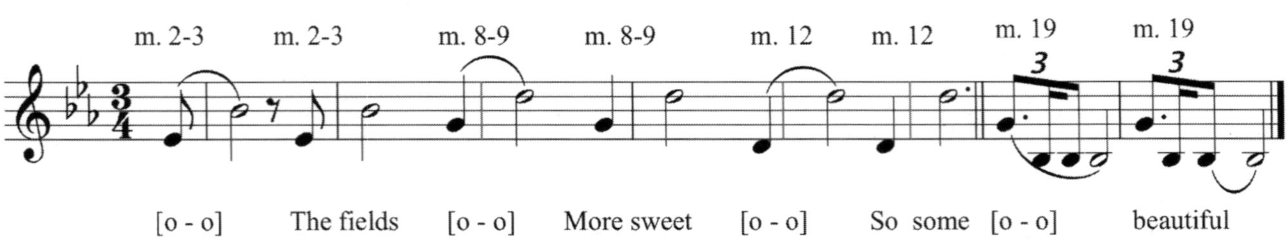

Diction and Articulation

To maintain a relaxed position of the jaw, hum the melody while chewing. The jaw should not be forced, but must relax with each movement. After practicing this, notice the released feeling in the jaw. Next, speak/chew the text with that same feeling. Finally, sing the melody, remembering the relaxation that was discovered in the exercises.

Phonetic Transcription of the Text

The	**fields**	**are**	**full**	**of**	**summer**	**still**
[ðʌ	fildz	ɑɐ̯	fʊl	ɑv	'sʌm.ɐ	stɪl]

And	**breathe**	**again**	**upon**	**the**	**air**
[ænd	bɹið	ə.'gɛn	ə.'pɑn	ði	ɛɐ̯]

From	**brown**	**dry**	**side**	**of**	**hedge**	**and**	**hill**
[fɹʌm	bɹa:ʊn	dɹa:ɪ	sa:ɪd	ɑv	hɛd͡ʒ	ænd	hɪl]

More	**sweetness**	**than**	**the**	**sense**	**can**	**bear.**
[mɔɐ̯	'swit.nəs	ðæn	ðʌ	sɛn*t*s	kæn	bɛɐ̯]

So	**some**	**old**	**couple**	**who**	**in**	**youth**
[so:ʊ	sʌm	o:ʊld	'kʌ.pəl	hu	ɪn	juθ]

With	**love**	**were**	**filled**	**and**	**overfull,**
[wɪð	lʌv	wɛɐ̯	fɪld	ænd	'o:ʊ.vɐ.fʊl]

And	**loved**	**with**	**strength**	**and**	**loved**	**with**	**truth,**
[ænd	lʌvd	wɪθ	stɹɛŋ*k*θ	ænd	lʌvd	wɪθ	tɹuθ]

In	**heavy**	**age**	**are**	**beautiful.**
[ɪn	'hɛ.vi	e:ɪd͡ʒ	ɑɐ̯	'bju.tɪ.fəl]

Late Summer

Edward Shanks

Peter Warlock
(1894-1930)

Lento-molto tranquillo

11
rit. molto
12
13
So some old cou - ple who in youth With
mf
p
*this measure edited from original
14
15
16
love were filled and o - ver - full, And loved with strength and loved with
17
18
19
20
truth, In heav-y age are beau - ti - ful.
cantabile

21
22
23
tr
24
3
25

La Rachelina

Aria from *La Molinara*
Giovanni Paisiello

Respiration and Support

To assist with consistent breath flow, sing the melody using the syllable [fla].

Resonance

Practice speaking with slightly protruded lips, lifted cheekbones, and a smile behind the eyes to assist with resonance. It may be helpful to watch yourself in a mirror or with the camera on your phone.

Phonation

Create the shape of the vowel in the vocal tract with no sound but with a gentle whisper. Bring the vocal folds gently together and practice the pure vowels [a], [e], [i], [o] and [u]. This will feel like a soft grunt and prepares the onset in the environment of the vowel shape.

Registration

This exercise assists in balancing registration.

Diction and Articulation

This exercise uses syllables that combine various vowels and consonants, which will provide an excellent bridge between the vocalise and song text.

Phonetic Transcription and Translation of the Text

La Rachelina, molinarina,
[la ra.k ɛ.ˈli:.na mo.li.na.ˈɾi:.na]
Rachelina, maid of the mill

il suo signore,
[il su:o sinˈɲo:.ɾe]
his lord,

viene a inchinar,
[ˈvjɛ:.ne a in.ki:.ˈnar]
come and bend down,

più vi direi
[pju vi di.ˈɾe:i]
I would tell you more

ma nò, ma non conviene,
[ma nɔ ma non kɔn.ˈvjɛ:.ne]
but no, but it's not suitable,

che so, vorrei
[ke so vɔr.ˈrɛ:i]
I know, I wish,

nò, non, sta bene,
[nɔ, non sta ˈbɛ:.ne]
but, no, it's fine,

son schietta, vergognosetta.
[son ˈskjɛt.ta ver.go.ɲo.ˈzɛt.ta]
I am sincere, shy

e la modestia, tacer mi fà.
[e la mo.ˈdes.tja ta.ˈtʃer mi fa]
and modest, I will keep silent.

La Rachelina

from *La molinara*

Guiseppe Palomba

Giovanni Paisiello
(1740-1816)

Andantino ♩ = 80

Un po' mosso ♩= 92
nar: più vi di - re - i, ma non con - vie - ne, che
pp
leggero
so più vi di - re - i ma non, ma non sta be - ne. Son schiet - ta,
f
p
schiet - ta, ver - go - gno - set - ta, e la mo - de - stia ta-

Più mosso =104
cer mi fa. Piu vi di - re - i, ma non con -
Più mosso ♩=104
vie - ne, che so, vor - re - i ma non sta be - ne.
rall.
rall.
Tempo I ♩ = 80
La Ra - che - li - na mo - li - na - ri - na il suo si -
Tempo I ♩=80

Un po' mosso ♩=92
gno - re vie - ne a in - chi - nar. Son schiet - ta, schiet - ta, ver
Un po' mosso ♩=92
go - gno - set - ta, e la mo - de - stia ta - cer, ta - cer mi
Più mosso ♩ = 104
p
fa. Più vi di - re - i ma non, ma non con - vie - ne,
Più mosso ♩=104
pp

rall
61
62
63
64
che so, vor - re - i, no, no, no, non sta ben...
Tempo I ♩ = 80
65
66
67
68
69
La Ra - che - li - na mo - li - na - ri - na il suo si-
Tempo I ♩=80
p
3
3
70
71
72
73
74
f
gno - re vie - ne a in - chi - na - re; il suo si - gno - re
mf

p
75
76
77
78
vie - ne a in - chi - na - re
il suo si - gno - re
pp
79
poco rall.
80
81
vie - ne a in - chi - nar.
3
3
pp
rall.

Thou Shalt Bring Them In

Oratorio Aria from *Israel in Egypt*
George Frederic Handel

Respiration and Support

Dynamic and flexible breath is essential for proper support. Sing the melismas on [v], feeling flexibility in the ribs and the abdominal muscles, and repeat with the text.

Resonance

The English language is consonant-heavy. In this aria, words with many consonants are set to notes with short rhythmic values. For example, in the first phrase *shalt, bring* and *them* are set to shorter notes. Speak these words slowly, making the vowels long and the consonants as quick as possible, which will help to create consistent and even resonance when singing.

Phonation

To ensure that phonation is flexible, practice singing a tone with, without, and again with vibrato. Singers might make a stylistic choice to sing without vibrato in baroque repertoire. This exercise prevents pressed phonation. Practice singing the flexible phonation, and then transition to the vocal line, retaining that flexibility.

Registration

This oratorio aria helps the singer to work through the lower *passaggio*. To allow for an easy transition through this region, maintain a slightly rounded lip position with a released jaw when descending. For example, if the word "mountain" is spread, the transition will be difficult. Practice the melisma on "mountain" on [o], and then remember the shape of [o] when singing the word.

Diction and Articulation

Shadow vowels may be necessary between two consonants, which can help to create flexible articulation. Speak slowly, adding a shadow vowel between these words. Gradually increase the speed, and as the articulators become more flexible, the shadow vowel may be removed. For example:

Shalt [ə] bring
And [ə] plant

Thou Shalt Bring Them In

from *Israel in Egypt*

G. F. Handel
(1658-1759)

- - tain of Thine in - her-it- ance, in the place, oh
p dolce
Lord, which Thou hast made, which Thou hast made for Thee to
r.h.
dwell in, for Thee to dwell in, to dwell
cresc.
cresc.

tranquillo
in, in the
dim.
sanc - tu - a - ry, oh Lord,
mp
which Thy hands have e - stab - - - - - -

tranquillo sempre
cresc.
lish - ed, in the sanc -
cresc.
mf
p
tu - a - - - - - ry
p dolce
mp
p
which Thy hands have e - stab - - - lish - ed, which Thy
più lento
p
più lento

96
97
98
99
100
101
102
103
hands have___ e-stab-lish - ed.
a tempo
mp
104
105
106
107
108
109
110
mf
dim.

Sample Rubric for Grading Repertoire

Scale of 1-5
0-20 points easy, 20-40 points moderate, 40-60 points difficult

Technical Issue Addressed	Problem Solving Questions	Scale 1-5
ACCOMPANIMENT	Is the accompaniment utilitarian, supportive, independent, etc.? Is the accompaniment part of the story line? Descriptive e.g. water figures, spinning wheel, etc.?	
CHARACTERIZATION/ACTING	Is the character appropriate to the student's dramatic capacity or life experiences? Will the student benefit from portraying this type of character?	
DICTION/ARTICULATION	Consideration of challenging consonant clusters. Closed position or difficult consonants on challenging pitches? Student's knowledge of French, Italian, Russian, German, etc. language or diction?	
DYNAMICS	Is the singer expected to sing a pianissimo high note? Are the markings pedagogically helpful (e.g. crescendo on sustained notes to assist in breath energy and/or vibrancy?)	
MELISMATIC PHRASES	Beginner or advanced melismas/melismatic phrases present? Appoggiatura? Dotted rhythms?	
MUSICAL CONSIDERATIONS	Through composed? Strophic? Accessible harmonic language? Tonal? An enjoyable melody?	
RANGE/TESSITURA	How are high notes approached—dramatically? Is the range too vast? Is the tessitura too low or high? Can a young singer sit in that particular part of the voice for that long without fatiguing?	
REGISTRATION	Does the piece assist in working through *passaggio* issues? Will the student carry weight up? Helpful vowels in an underdeveloped part of the student's voice? Etc.	
RESPIRATION	Are phrase lengths accessible? Will the breaths allow for renewal of positioning?	
TEXT SETTING	Syllabic, Patter Song, Lyric? Does the text setting assist in memorization?	
VOWELS/VOWEL SEQUENCES	Observation of vowels in *passaggio*. Will vowel patterns assist in correcting vocal faults forward to back, tongue position, etc.?	
WORDS: POETRY/LYRICS/LIBRETTO	Is this accessible poetry? Is the story age appropriate? Will the text make the memorization process difficult?	